I can ride on a balloon...

Copyright: Pollywoguen Creations - 2025
All rights reserved by Robert Carr
ISBN Hardback 978 1 959707 29 5
ISBN Softback 978 1 959707 30 1
Edited by Aubree Carr
Produced by Ingram Sparks
Website:
robertcarrpollywoguencreations.com
Instagram: Pollywoguen Creations
Uno Series

I CAN AND SO CAN YOU

Written and illustrated by Robert Carr

My name is Uno. What is your name? _____ .

I can stand on my head.

I can make my own bed.

I can outrun a bee.

I can hang from a tree.

I can swing from a vine.

I can climb a great pine.

I can thread worms on hooks.

I can read many books.

I can hide in a cave.

I can ride a big wave.

I can make my feet into talking puppets.

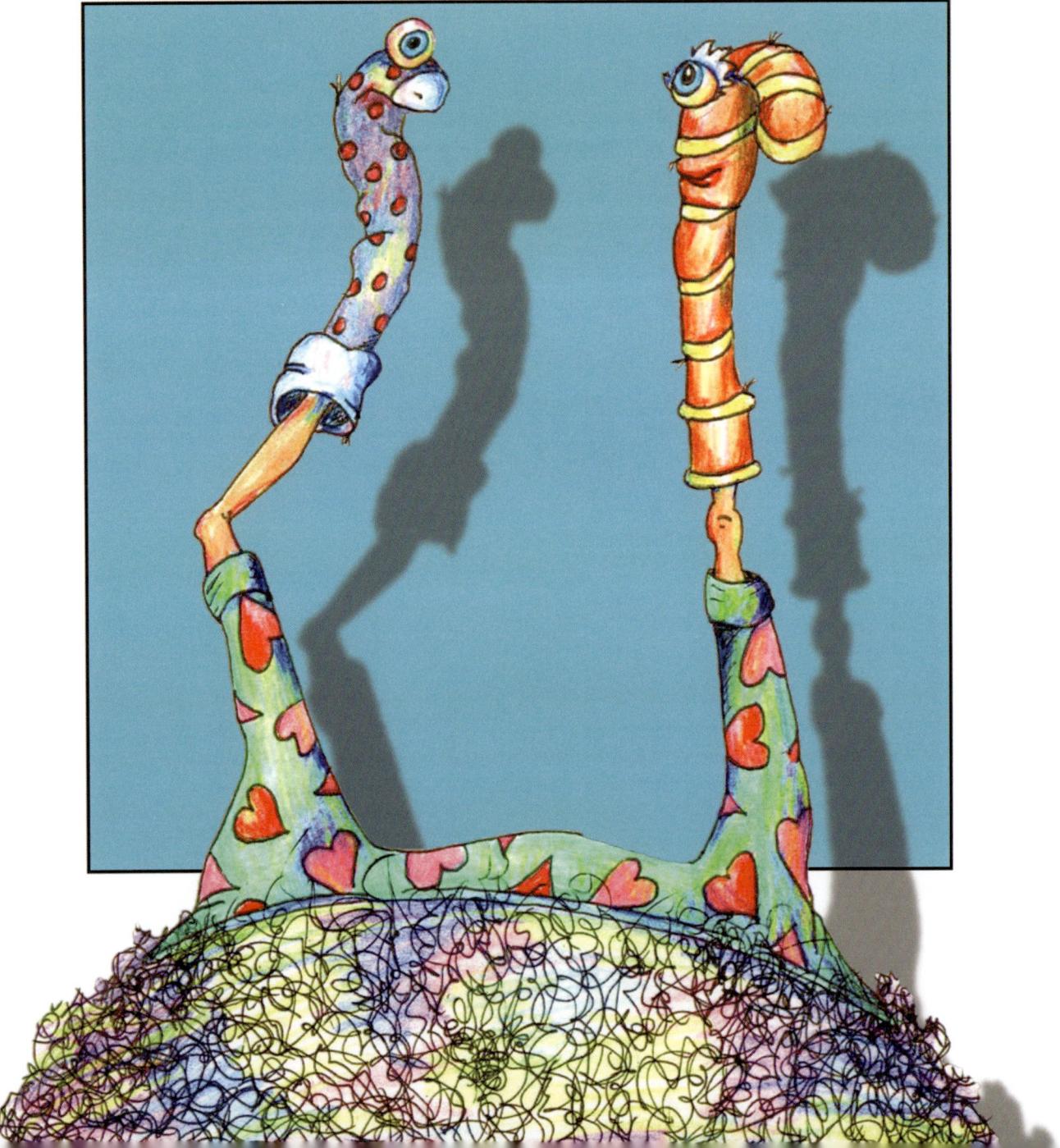

I can scoop up dinner with two buckets.

I can ride a donkey.

I can act like a monkey.

I can dance for an hour.

I can build a tall tower.

I can pick mushrooms with my toes.

I can gather corn with the crows.

I can match all my socks.

I can lift heavy rocks.

I can break into song.

I can also be wrong.

I can skate on ice.

I can also be nice.

I can be friends with a gnome.

I can write a poem.

I can. I will

www.ingramcontent.com/pod-product-compliance
Lightning Source LLC
Chambersburg PA
CBRC091204010526
44107CB00021B/1240